PAIN CONQUERS ALL
By: Tramika Giles

Copyright © 2016 by Tramika Giles

All Biblical texts in this publication are quoted from the Bible.

All rights reserved. This book or any portion thereof may not be reproduced or used in any manner whatsoever without the express written permission of the publisher except for the use of brief quotations in a book review.

Printed in the United States of America

First Printing, 2016

ISBN-13: 978-0997485707

ISBN-10: 0997485701

Pataskity Publishing

Augusta, Georgia

Phone: 706-303-8771

Dedications

To my grandmother, Rosabell Moore, I thank you for being more than a grandma. Thank you for always loving me past my pain. Your life has taught me no matter the pain if I fight through in prayer, I will conquer all.

~~~~~~~

I dedicate this book to my daughters, Destiny & Jazsmin. What can I say, other than thank you for being a part of life's roller coaster with me? You two, have without regard shared me as I've pursued my destiny while effecting many with possibilities. You two loved me despite the long work hours, practice hours, and the many of people attracted and connected in our lives regardless if they stayed or not. I am so blessed by God to have because he loaned me you two.

I promised you both that I vow to make our lives better. Thank you two for being my motivation and inspiration. You two along with my Dad "Jimmie, my brothers, my mom, "Rip Myme" and Uncle Eddie and many others believed in me no matter my process! I promised you all, that without fail, we shall recover all! I'm privileged to be called "Ma" by the two of you, but an honor to call you my daughters.

~~~~~~~

To Roderick, Rionna, Paulette, Bishop Michael Shackleford, I thank you for all your time invested in this project. I am forever grateful to you. Thank you for your loyalty and friendships forever cherished.

~~~~~~~

In memory of my mother, Ida Mae "Joann" Giles and my uncle Eddie Moore, may you continue to rest in the Heavens~

Confronting catastrophes, or life hardships of any sort, can be very irritable. Nevertheless, during despair and agony, you can find the strength and endurance to move forward. With surrendering and allowing God's help, along with the help of those He has assigned in your path, you will indeed receive the necessary empowerment to conquer all.

"For I reckon that the sufferings of this present time are not worthy to be compared with the glory which shall be revealed in us."

Romans 8:18

Introduction

Confronting catastrophes, or life hardships of any sort, can be very irritable. Nevertheless, during despair and agony, you can find the strength and endurance to move forward. With surrendering and allowing God's help, along with the help of those He has assigned in your path, you will indeed receive the necessary empowerment to conquer all.

The enemy within yourself just maybe taunting you saying: "You can never get through this storm, trial, or test." You may even be fighting the thought or feelings of depression, frustration, bitterness, resentment, suffering, fear, doubt, worry, and even the spirit of confusion and violation. Beloved, rest for sure, these are all normal responses to life disappointments and failures. But, please know, you can overcome!

1 Peter 5:10

"And after you have suffered a little while, the God of all grace (who imports all blessings and favor), who has called you to His (own) eternal glory in Christ Jesus, will Himself complete and make you what you ought to be, establish and ground you securely, and strengthen, and settle you."

As difficult as this life may appear, you are not alone. The Bible declares that God says, "Lo, I am with thee always, even until the end of time." My sister, my brother, please realize that God loves you, and He is concerned about what you are facing. The devil is a liar. God hears your cries and He sees your pain. Surely, you were created for such a time as this!

Exodus 3:7-8

"And the Lord said, I have surely seen the affliction of My people who are in Egypt, and have heard their cry because of their taskmasters and oppressors; for I know their sorrows and sufferings and trials. And I have come down to deliver them out of the hand and power of the Egyptians and to bring them up out of that land to a land good and large, a land flowing with milk and honey (a land of plenty) – to the land of the Canaanite, the Hittite, the Amorite, the Perizzite, the Hivite, and the Jebusite."

It is my prayer that the start to my writing journey will provide comfort, strength, encouragement, and healing for you and your family, and that through these pages you will rediscover extraordinary faith, and the bountiful blessing of victory that only He can give. May God graciously bless you and keep you always in His tender care on life's journey!

"Have not I command you? Be strong, vigorous, and very courageous. Be not afraid, neither be dismayed, for the Lord your God is with you wherever you go."

Joshua 1:9

"And God shall wipe away all tears from their eyes; and there shall be no more death, neither sorrow, nor crying, neither shall there be any more pain: for the former things are passed away."

Revelation 21:4

You Are Not Alone

Let your character or moral disposition be free from love of money [including greed, avarice, lust, and craving for earthly possessions] and be satisfied with your present [circumstances and with what you have]; for He [God] Himself has said, "I will not in any way fail you nor give you up nor leave you without support. [I will] not, [I will] not, [I will] not in any degree leave you helpless nor forsake nor let [you] down (relax My hold on you)! [Assuredly not!]

Joshua 1:5

I will never forget the day that changed my family's life forever. It was a nice hot summer day. My dad, along with my brothers and his baseball players, packed his station wagon up and rode to Mullins, South Carolina to play baseball. I was sitting on my grandmother's porch and I heard a loud yell coming from across the street! Cecelia was screaming walking to her mom's house – yelling no! No!

Lord, Why? I will never forget that cry! Then Jason walked up to me and said, "They found Angie in Black River." Even though I was only eleven years old, I remember using some of my grandma's words on him; I dare not write them for the sake of my deliverance. Then cars came out of nowhere, and started pulling up and down Jones Avenue. I remembered being called into the house. My mom told me to stay at my grandma's house because she had to go get my dad. I was young, but not dumb. "Myme", which is what I called my mom. I asked: "How are you going to get my dad? You can't drive his truck!" Needless to say, she learned that day! After my parents got back, I knew it had to be true. When my dad got out of his car, I heard those same words from earlier, but this time it was with anger and sorrow mixed together. "Nooooo! Noooooooo!" Then my dad said, "Lord, no, no not my child!" For all you who may not know, my sister was murdered! Days later, my nephew, only two years old was found in the same river his mom was tossed in. (This story will be written in further details in another book.)

Can you imagine what devastation such act placed on my family, her mom's family, and my nephew's father's family? Let alone the small town of Andrews, South Carolina. Our families and community thrust instantly into the darkness and despair of our loss leaving the lack of trust in families across small towns. Thus, my family sought comfort and serenity among our brothers, sisters, and their children.

Many family and friends from different states were affected by this evil murder, and horrific tragedy of a mother and her son. Some would suggest never being able to recover from this catastrophe. Despite my pain, I can say, I'm sorry my sister and nephew's life was snatched away, but God knew the lesson only he can teach; that lesson is forgiveness.

I remember writing to my sister's brother, I did not ask any questions, it was simple, I said to him – I forgive you. Even though you lost your sister, and you are not my biological brother, I want you to know I can never replace our sister, but I can continue to love you as she would, so you still have a sister. Let me take this moment to explain to you, I don't expect everyone to understand what took place the day I wrote that letter. Till this day, I don't see him as a murderer, killer, etc. I saw him as a young man then and a man now who has a soul worth saving – another soul.

I can only imagine the pain, hurt, and disbelief our families felt by this violence that stroke us unaware. Yes, many may have felt that they've been abandoned by God, but ultimately God has the final say so.

I can only think of the various families that this violence and tragedies struck because they may be feeling as if they also have been abandoned by God. Despite what trouble has hit your life regardless if it is calamity, hurt from of a loved one, unbelievable medical diagnosis, repossessions of your home, car, and even land, you may have gotten fired from the job you were loyal to for years; It may be that you are experiencing your very own intense storm. Know that God has not forgotten you!

David, wrote in Psalms 119:71:

"It is good for me that I have been afflicted, that I might learn Your statues!"

Others may be feeling a little inadequate as if the entire world is against them, and there is no end at the tunnel. Indeed, times like these will lend you into disbelief that you are alone. You, my friend, are not alone. Even during unfortunate and unspeakable pain God is with you. I know you may not feel his presence, but He is near. God, is right there. He assures us that he will never leave nor forsake us. With that being said, wherever you are, God is there with you. Entering into, the midst of, and even existing during your crucial, hard times, pain, sorrow, and overwhelming circumstances, God is with you, never, (and I do mean) never losing sight of you, even in the tough times, your tough time may be a failed marriage, a broken heart, sickness in your body, even a failed ministry, guess what? God is still there, to mend every broken piece of your life, embracing you, letting you know that He is so much greater in you than any detrimental catastrophe in your life. Psalms 46:11 states: "God is a very present help in the time of a storm, trouble, or catastrophe." Trust his word, and know that is he there with you all times in your life.

"The LORD of hosts is with us; the God of Jacob is our refuge."

Psalm 46:11

Can I remind you that the Lord knows in great detail the devastation caused by every chaotic catastrophe? He understands the grief and burden acquainted with pain and agony. I know you may be asking, "How does Tramika know God understands?" I know he does because at a young age, Ms. Dapheny Scott, taught me in Sunday school, that God is all knowing, he's an all wise God. After all, Jesus himself endured suffering.

Isaiah 53: 3-5

He was despised and rejected and forsaken by men, a man of sorrows and pains, and acquainted with grief and sickness, and like one from whom men hide their faces He was despised, and we did not appreciate His worth or have any esteem for Him. Surely, he has borne our griefs (sicknesses, weaknesses, and distresses) and carried our sorrows and pains (of punishment), yet we (ignorantly) considered him stricken, smitten, and afflicted by God (as if with leprosy).

Matthew 8:17

But he was wounded for our transgressions, he was bruised for our guilt and inequities, the chastisement (needful to obtain) peace and well-being for us, was upon him, and with the stripes (that wounded) him we are healed and made whole. Praise Jesus, here is where you should thank the Lord. Go ahead, I did! He knew pain. In fact, he is your pain. It doesn't matter what your pain is or was rather its rejection or abandonment, he knew pain. You are not alone!

Matthew 27:46

And about the ninth hour (three o'clock) Jesus cried about with a loud voice, Eli, Eli, lama sabachthani? – that is, My God, My God, why have you abandoned me (leaving me helpless, forsaking and failing me in my need)? You are not alone! Declare it with me, you are not alone!

Psalms 139:8

"If I ascend up into Heaven, thou art there's if I make my bed in Hell, behold, thou art there." You see, the quicker you realize this the sooner you will know for certain that you are not alone. The Lord is everywhere always; He knows that you are suffering. He sees the intense pain and he hears the cries of your heart, mind and soul. Trust and believe, God is near thee in such a time as this!

My friend, the Lord cares deeply and passionately for you, just as He did for my father, and is concerned about every aspect of your being even those areas that burden your heart.

2 Corinthians 12:9

But he said to me, my grace (my favor and loving kindness and mercy) is enough for you (sufficient) against any danger and enables you to bear the trouble manfully), for my strength and power are made perfect (fulfilled and completed) and show themselves most effective in (your) weakness.

1 Peter 5:7

Casting the whole of your care (all your anxieties, all your worries, all your concerns, once and for all) on him, for he cares for you affectionately and cares about you watchfully.

Psalms 55:22

How reassuring and comforting to know that the Lord really does care for you and he is working it out just for you. It may appear that everything around you is shaking and disappearing to the core, but God compassionately loves you and that love is everlasting. You are not alone!

In 2011, it was a year of great loss, tremendous difficulties, more failures than success, believed God for things in 2011 that never happened. I stepped completely out if my carapace and decided to love people with my whole heart. Needless to say, I have trusted steadily and effortlessly only to get burned in the end. I had to make some drastic decisions about my life and my destiny, choices that have led me into an enormous pit I've ever known. Just that year alone, I walked through the most severe, vigorous, and unpleasant identity crisis of my life. And if the truth was to be told, I was ready to make my exit!

First and foremost, it doesn't matter how many people admire or think highly of you, or have been encouraged, motivated and inspired by you when you go home to intense despair, accompanied by severe depression that grip the very depths of your being. No doubt, I have been quite successful at ministering, encouraging, and inspiring others and an absolute total failure at encouraging, ministering, and inspiring myself. In 2011, I've had the opportunity to stand on both sides of the tracks. In fact, I had experienced the presence of God on various levels, God's superlative, ultimate, utmost power commissioning and thrusting me to move forward. His grace overriding despair out of my life, his love navigating me to the safest place in the world, which is Him. Nevertheless, I've also experienced extreme lows where I purposed to question whether or not God was with me. A road so rough it voided my option of progressing or advancing forward. A pain so deep it became mental and physical which incapacitated me with an emotion beyond words.

One of the most significant lesson's I have learned during my transition is that you hand the devil his championship ring when you cease from obeying God's word and you refrain from praying. It is the adversary's job to cause you to successfully abort your prayer life triumphantly preventing you from communicating with God by robbing your will to avail, your ambition to triumph and your power to fight back. The adversary's logic for robbing your joy is uncomplicated, not difficult, and straightforward, he understands your joy is the birthplace of your strength. Of course he thinks he's intelligent, overwhelmingly manipulative, and subtle, the only way he can successfully rob your joy is to observe and acquire information about you, and keep tabs on the things that bring you joy, happiness, and then plots to snatch them away from you! Let me help out right here, that's why it is very necessary and imperative that as believers we find our peace, happiness, and joy in the Lord, not fame, man, money, etc., the adversary can take everything else from us, but he cannot take God. Unfortunately, if your happiness is in your house, may be your vehicle, perhaps your job, your bank account, hobby, play station, or even your favorite show, and the list goes on and on. Beware, I promise you the adversary will definitely target and launch an attack in those areas. Let me ask, what will you do when that dream home is foreclosed on, that nice shiny, clean vehicle is reposed, how about when the business fails, perhaps after pledging your loyalty to that company, only to be fired without legitimate cause, maybe your bank account is depleted, and all that talent you got is overlooked because of where you came from, the hobby you love so much but it's too expensive to maintain, and your favorite show have been cancelled? I know, I know. This may appear insignificant and simple, but I came to realize it's the small flicker that may cause a large explosion!

"Beloved, think it not strange concerning the fiery trial which is to try you, as though some strange thing happened unto you:

But rejoice, inasmuch as ye are partakers of Christ's sufferings; that, when his glory shall be revealed, ye may be glad also with exceeding joy."

1 Peter 4:12-4:13

Contrary to popular opinions, I personally have been in a place where I have literally greeted Jesus in the sanctuary only to go home in to grief the adversary in my room. He would wait graciously and meekly for me, clenching at the moment to abduct, and snatch everything I just acquired in the presence of the Lord. The fact of the matter is I never lock my room door. Despite the fact, I lived with my brother, he had no key, and if I was to lock the door – just like the adversary- my brother could find a way to get in. Considerately and with all due respect, he never entered in my room unless he was invited. The only people allowed in my room, my territory, my personal space, are only those who I invite in. I have very few friends who were always welcomed, of course my brothers and daughters don't ever have to ask, they are indeed privy to my confidentiality, and it's alright with me. In fact, there was never a need for discussion, or permission.

Different from my room, the question arises, who solicited the adversary of my soul in? Hmmm, let's get straight to the point of this experience. Have you ever wondered really who invited the enemy, the adversary, the devil, the demons, of your being in. I remember, my dad telling me, I was four years old and before I ever talked. Needless to say, that explained why I attended speech classes my first year of elementary school. With that being said, can you only imagine seconds, minutes, hours, days, weeks, months, and years being silent. Others, may have assumed your responses even when it literally wasn't. What am I saying… your silence can often be misconceived as agreement! For this matter, it can become extremely treacherous! It doesn't matter if your door is bolted down in the natural, but it was open in the spirit. Listen to me, that adversary observed relentlessly waiting for his grand opportunity to enter, and me, without acknowledgment, gave him leeway in. Sporadically, it's not at all the enormous, noticeable things that we automatically assume to have gone wrong, like sexual desires and perversions, homosexuality, murders with your tongue instead of guns. I've came to realize as author Henry Jones said, "It's more than a notion." It's the smaller things that humans tend to overlook in the overall fast pace of everyday life. Please remember that what you tend to disregard, the devil emphasizes on.

Him being the conspiring, subtle, and sly little demon he is ciphered in on my plans. Between kids, work, and coaching, I had become extremely overwhelmed and exhausted, with that being said, prayer became less and before long, I wasn't praying at all. It doesn't take a rocket scientist to know, it was at that very second, I handed the adversary my spare key. With fever to no prayer going on in my life, energy was zapped, and you could tell I was literally running out of oil, my oil level was not even registering, but yet I kept going. It's like when you hit I-95, or I-77, open highway, you don't want to exit off even though you know you need to add a quart of oil, or the empty light on, but you're riding, jamming to the music, the ride is still progressing smoothly, you pushing it because you know you are almost at your exit. I'm sorry, but when you have that bed of yours in view with the remote waiting for Law and Order to come on, who wants to interrupted? But, you've seen plenty of signs advertising Speedway, B.P., Exxon, and QT Quick Stop stations off the next exit, here you become bargaining with yourself, "Aww man, I can make it to the next exit." Are you following me? Literally, I'm getting the bed as comfortable as possible for the adversary, have a seat, the bed is nice and cozy for you! My car officially has locked up, it's worse than being on E, I can't do anything. I can't move any further, in fact the key won't even turn over. My car is at a complete standstill, sad thing about it is that there is absolutely nothing I can do at this point, not because I don't want to, but because I don't trust driving knowing the car needed oil, and gas, and smarty me… run out of both! It's a very uncompromising, unfavorable, situation when you choose to be disobedient to what you know is the right thing to do. You see, it wasn't the car's fault – It was me! I'd seen all the things, I knew it needed oil and gas, but I kept going, "I can make it…." Listen to me, a car without oil and gas will eventually lock up. A person without an identity will eventually fall prey to the adversary! I don't care how anointed you think you are, how powerful you assume you are, or how gifted you think yourself to be, a person without submission to God, to prayer, to fasting, etc., you are lost! No doubt, I handed over the keys and rode out with the adversary, daily! What you must realize that it wasn't an overnight thing, several weeks and moths I would drive without checking the oil, water, or servicing my car. Don't ever think that you're so saved that the adversary is just going to leave you alone. And the Lord said to Satan," Have you considered about my servant Tramika?" You don't have a Do Not Disturb pass because you think that you are anointed. I realized early – the more you love God, the more you are a target. The adversary awaits to discredit you – He resents you – he wants you dead! The greater the anointed, the greater the agony! I knew the adversary wanted to kill every dream, every goal, every ambition, every desire. He wanted me dead! Not vulnerable, not breakable, not delicate, DEAD! You understand me? DEAD!!!!!

You see, even though the adversary isn't welcomed with open arms, the second you give him a little space, he comes in, props his feet up and becomes relaxed! I would attend services, and would be on a spiritual high. But, the second I left, the adversary awaited to greet me, in what should've been my safe haven. The old folks use to say, if it's not one thing, it's another. The more I tried, it seemed the depression of the loss of my mother he smothered me with memories of a failed relationship. With constant thoughts of why me! I felt like I was holding on to Heaven with Hell on my back. Discouragement will override my thoughts. It was so persistent in echoing, it will never work, you can't be loved, your business fail, ministry fail, it just not for you, lies being told, you might as well throw in the towel! It seemed as if my past would not let me pass. Constant reminders of my past from divorce, all the way back to the most traumatic childhood experiences it was at that point, I became overwhelmed. More days than none I would cry, seem like God was against me and the adversary definitely didn't celebrate me. You see, because I was so empty, I entertained the adversary constant torment. Sad to say, I became so weak, having no energy to even fight Him back. Although many prophesize this abundant future for me, I was too distraught to even fantasize abundant living, it just wasn't in my view. I couldn't see – the book, the souls, the wealth nor good health. I saw defeat, failure, and lack, and pity. The more the adversary spoke, it seems he had my undivided attention. Seems it was becoming obvious, I went to church, there was always a word, I would have the word clearly! Most of the services I attend, the word was always on point, but then I get home, the only voice I could hear is the adversary. He was in my car in my home, in my room, in my thoughts. Simply, he was in my head. Listen to me, you know there's a problem when the voice of the adversary becomes louder than the voice of God in your ear. The adversary steadily demolished my peace, my joy, my self- worth, my self-esteem, my motivation, my drive until finally I hit rock bottom. When I say rock bottom, I mean just that. No money, no job, family and friends turned their backs on me, church seems it was like a vacant run down house. Who pays attention to an abandoned, house? You know the house with paint peeled, a leaking roof, yard wasn't in tack, if a good wind blew, the house would just fall down. Who's going to invest into that unpleasant run down house?

Who wants a woman who's divorced, has two kids? Who wants that woman who preached but gave up on her own ministry? Who's going to invest in a woman who doesn't know who she is, who sat contemplating which way she would take her own life? The truth is, if you spend enough time with anyone, it's only matter of the time before you begin to act of do as they do. Obviously, because I allow the adversary in my space, I began to speak like the adversary, I was roommate with the adversary. He spoke failure, I spoke failure. He spoke negative, I spoke negative. He spoke depression, I spoke depression. It's like we were acquainted with each other, and there was no dispute we concurred with each other. Caution: Hazardous Zone! I was distraught, that it came to the point where my spirit within me, fainted.

"He that dwelleth in the secret place of the most High shall abide under the shadow of the Almighty."

Psalm 91:1

When I heard God, I didn't trust him, help me Jesus! When he spoke to me, I didn't believe him. I had no confidence, I questioned his will and purpose for my life. I protested everything he said out of disbelief. What's sad about all this, is that he never gave me a reason to doubt him – then or now – but yet I doubted him out of bitterness, frustration, and define association with his greatest rebel.

Certainly, I could identify with Jacob when Laban tricked him. Also Elijah when he fled for his life because of Jezebel. I can relate to David when he said, "day and night I have only tears for food, while my enemies continuously taunt me, saying, "Where is this God of yours?"" Safe to say, I felt Naomi's pain, I concur with her when she says, "I went away full, but the Lord has brought me back empty." Why call me Tramika? The Lord has afflicted me; the Almighty has brought misfortune upon me. Have you ever wanted to scream so loud with the hopes of feeling better? Apart of me, know how it must have felt when Jesus said," Eli Eli Lama Sabachthani!" Even how the blind man felt when he yelled, "Son of David, have mercy on me!" I'm telling you, the pain within my soul couldn't be articulated.

In all honesty, after living this way a few tears, I greeted 2012 with great despair, but I promise you, it took no leaps and bounds on God's end to dig me out of "a horrible pit." I will never forget, the night of New Year's Eve, I heard a sermon the snatched me out of my despair, it was entitled "I survived one of the worst seasons of my life". Oh my God, I knew it was for me because I wasn't even supposed to be in town that day, but I had to be there. I began to listen to the bishop, taking notes, as the tears rolled down my eyes. I began to realize, it means absolutely nothing to win in the church and lose in my room. As I traveled back to my destination, tears rolling, I knew it was going to be a long morning. One conversation with the king knitted to my heart, and an authentic encounter with God in the wee hours of the morning met me where I was. That's right, he met me in my pain, my frustration, my bitterness, my brokenness and brought me to this place of surrender! Now, I comprehend what Daniel meant when he said, "I saw the Lord always in my presence; for He is at my right hand, so that I will not be shaken." I may have not arrived but I know I believe God, my faith has been restored and I can surely say in thy presence, "Oh Lord is the fullness of thy joy!"

The adversary is counting on you to throw in the towel. He is counting on you to lose insight. He is counting on you to fail. In spite of what has transpired in your life, it is time you, as Pastor John P. Kee often quotes, "Own your past. Allow your present to become your witness."

Here's my version of John 10:28-30 –

"And I give Tramika eternal life, and Tramika shall never lose it or perish throughout her ages. (To all eternity

Tramika shall never by any means be destroyed.) And no one is able to snatch Tramika out of my hand."

vs. 29 "Tramika Father (Which art in Heaven). Who has given Tramika to me, is greater and mightier than all (else), and no one is able to snatch Tramika out the Father's hand."

vs. 30 "I and the Father are one!"

I GOT MY OIL BACK!!!!!

www.ingramcontent.com/pod-product-compliance
Lightning Source LLC
Chambersburg PA
CBHW071316110426
42743CB00042B/2693